HOW TO KNOW SOMEONE DEEPLY

The Art of Relating with People Genuinely by Understanding Who they Really Are

James Edwards

All rights reserved. No part of this publication may be reproduced, distributed, or transmitted in any form or by any means, including photocopying, recording, or other electronic or mechanical methods, without the prior written permission of the publisher, except in the case of brief quotations embodied in critical reviews and certain other noncommercial uses permitted by copyright law.

Copyright © by James Edwards 2024

TABLE OF CONTENTS

INTRODUCTION

CHAPTER ONE

The Significance of Gaining Absolute Knowledge of People

CHAPTER TWO

The Bedrock of Genuine Relationship

CHAPTER THREE

The Fundamental Knowledge of Personality Traits and Temperaments

CHAPTER FOUR

The Necessity of Gaining Mastery of Emotional Intelligence

CHAPTER FIVE

The Relevance of Beliefs, Values, and Worldviews

CHAPTER SIX

The Fundamental Knowledge of Communication Styles

CHAPTER SEVEN

Developing Trust and Vulnerability

CHAPTER EIGHT

Developing Empathy and Compassion

CHAPTER NINE

The Necessity of Settling Conflict Effectively

CHAPTER TEN

The Value of Forgiveness and Restoration in Relationships

CHAPTER ELEVEN

Mutual Development in a Relationship

CONCLUSION

ABOUT THE AUTHOR

INTRODUCTION

An uncommon and valuable skill in a fast-moving digital society where relationships are typically made quickly and superficially is the skill of getting to know someone deeply. This book examines the complexities of human associations, analyzing the significant skill of connecting with others to a very high extent by realizing their inner nature.

This book offers a very great knowledge together with helpful advice for improving relationships at work, with friends, and with romantic partners. It provides a guideline for developing sincere bonds and deep partnerships.

Readers will go on an advancing route of self-observation and human relations through the well-presented studies in the pages of the book. You'll be learning the secrets to penetrating human comprehension and creating connections that go beyond outward manifestations.

Come along on this fascinating journey into the subconscious and conscious mind of humans to discover the true nature of people and how to relate to them authentically.

CHAPTER ONE

The Significance of Gaining Absolute Knowledge of People

There's a big difference in the human relationship experience between knowing someone on the surface and knowing them in depth. Merely superficial understanding only provides a casual glance at an individual's outermost layers. Deep knowledge, on the other hand, explores the many facets of their experiences, ideas, emotions, and personalities. We'll look at why getting to know someone well is important for developing authentic relationships in this chapter.

Four Reasons Sincere Relationships Are Important

Sincere relationships are essential to a happy existence. They offer a sense of understanding, encouragement, and intimacy that is incomparable to that of casual relationships. A pillar of trust and truth is established when you get to know someone well, and this opens the door to worthwhile communications. The following four factors indicate the value of sincere relationships:

1. Trust and Openness: Since it shows that you've invested the time and energy to get to know someone further than their outward appearance, deep knowledge promotes trust. When there is trust between two people, a safe place is created where they may both be honest, open up, and communicate their deepest feelings without fear of rejection.

2. Empathy and Compassion: Genuine empathy and compassion are developed via understanding someone. Understanding the experiences of someone else's life,

challenges, and victories makes it easier for you to sympathize with their feelings and offer sincere concern and assistance in return.

3. Resolving Conflicts: Any relationship will unfailingly encounter conflicts. But getting to know someone well helps you handle disagreements better. By determining the genesis of problems, improving your communication, and coming up with win-win solutions, you may fortify your relationship rather than weaken it.

4. Mutual Growth: Mutual growth is a result of intense knowledge. You can assist someone's personal growth path by getting to know their strengths, weaknesses, goals, and fears. In return, they can help you attain yours in reciprocation.

Five Advantages of Knowing Someone Deeply

1. Enhanced Communication: By encouraging openness, empathy, and attentive listening, intense knowledge of someone enhances communication. You may successfully modify your associations with others by being aware of their communication style, priorities, and affections.

2. Creating Genuine Relationships: Respect and understanding between people are the foundation of genuine relationships. A strong connection is formed with someone you know, one that goes beyond casual relationships and fosters enduring friendships, partnerships, and cooperative efforts.

3. Decreased Misunderstandings: Misunderstandings frequently result from inappropriate communication or a lack of comprehension. By understanding someone well, you reduce the likelihood of misunderstandings by perceiving their words and behaviors in light of their distinct personality and life experiences.

4. Support in Times of Need: Having an in-depth understanding of someone enables you to offer the person genuine assistance when he is going through a difficult period. Your comprehension makes it possible for you to assist them in a significant way, whether that is lending a sympathetic ear, helping them out practically, or providing emotional support.

5. Enhanced Emotional Intelligence: Gaining an in-depth understanding of other people makes you more emotionally intelligent. You get more proficient at interpreting nonverbal clues, more sensitive to emotions, and more skillful at managing delicate and complicated interpersonal interactions.

To put it simply, getting to know someone well is a continuous process that calls for empathy, curiosity, and a sincere hunger to relate on an honest level. It's about appreciating the richness of human differences and seeing behind the veil of our physical expressions. As you set out on this path, keep in mind that the benefits of real connections and understanding other people completely supersede the work involved.

CHAPTER TWO

The Bedrock of Genuine Relationship

In order to truly get to know someone and develop the skill of genuine human relations, we must first establish the groundwork for meaningful relationships. The two main foundations of self-awareness and empathy are examined in this chapter. Boosting genuine relationships and learning the true nature of people require cultivating empathy and understanding oneself.

The Four Principal Aspects of Self-Awareness

The foundation of sincere relationships is self-awareness. It entails being aware of your passions, thoughts, feelings, beliefs, and values in addition to your strengths and shortcomings. It is difficult to relate to people honestly when you don't have a firm grasp of who you are. The following are the four main aspects of self-awareness:

1. Acknowledging Your Originality: Being original is staying true to who you are rather than acting differently. It's embracing your individuality and admitting your shortcomings. Being genuine draws people who value you for your character, creating stronger bonds built on openness and confidence.

2. Discovering Your Inner World: Give yourself some time to reflect. Think back on your life's experiences, the impacts you had as a child, important connections, and turning points. You can learn a lot about your emotions and behavioral

patterns by examining your inner world and using journal writing, and mindfulness practices as helpful methods.

3. Making Your Beliefs and Values Clear: Determine your basic beliefs and values. What is most important to you? Which values direct your choices and behavior? Knowing your values enables you to make decisions that are consistent with who you really are, which promotes more satisfying relationships based on respect and common ground.

4. Understanding Your Prompts and Reactions: Recognize the words, circumstances, or behaviors that set off intense emotional reactions in you. These are your prompts. Knowing what your prompts are and why they influence you can help you behave thoughtfully instead of thoughtlessly, which will improve your relationships and interactions with people.

Four Principal Aspects of Empathy

The capacity to comprehend and experience another person's emotions is known as empathy. It entails putting oneself in another person's position, considering their mindset, and reacting in a kind and considerate manner. Four main aspects of empathy are as follows:

1. Promoting Empathetic Listening: Make an effort to actively listen throughout discussions. Pay close attention to the speaker's hidden messages, interests, and feelings. Pose inquiry-based questions, paraphrase to make sure you understand, and demonstrate empathy by expressing your own experiences without passing judgment.

2. Developing Perspective-Taking Skills: Consider things from the other person's point of view to understand their ideas, emotions, and experiences. Take into

account their upbringing, values, and way of life. It takes empathy to value other people's distinct perspectives without sticking to your own opinion.

3. Exhibiting Sincere Concern and Compassion: Show empathy with your words and deeds. Provide assistance, affirmation, and motivation to someone who is facing difficulties or disclosing their weaknesses. Demonstrate your sincere concern for their welfare and your willingness to listen and comprehend without passing judgment or offering advice.

4. Honoring Differences and Boundaries: Honor the distinctions and boundaries among people. Recognize that not everyone experiences emotions or shows them identically. Recognize how situational, cultural, and individual factors affect communication and relationships in order to promote an accepting and compassionate way of interacting with other people.

Building self-awareness and empathy lays the groundwork for genuine relationships and expanding your comprehension of other people. With the use of these fundamental abilities, you will be able to create relationships that are genuine, empathetic, and respectful of one another, adding rich experiences and important relationships to your life.

CHAPTER THREE

The Fundamental Knowledge of Personality Traits and Temperaments

Decoding someone's temperament and personality features is essential if we are to get to know them well and have a meaningful relationship with them. These characteristics influence how people view and engage with the environment, providing important illumination into their feelings, ideas, and actions. In order to improve our capacity for genuine interpersonal connection, let's explore the details of different personalities and temperamental variances.

Mastering the Big Five Personality Traits

A person's persistent recurring patterns of emotions, ideas, and actions that define their individuality are known as personality traits. These characteristics frequently show up regularly in a range of contexts, providing an insight into an individual's inner reality. There are many other personality models, however, the Big Five Personality Traits are among the most well-known:

1. Openness: This quality indicates how receptive a person is to novel situations, concepts, and viewpoints. People who score highly on openness are typically creative, inquisitive, and open to new ideas.

2. Conscientiousness: People who exhibit conscientiousness are well-organized, industrious, and dependable. They put accountability first, focus on the little things, and aim for success in whatever they do.

3. Extraversion: The degree of a person's friendliness, assertiveness, and excitement in social situations is known as extraversion. Extraverts like being around people, they flourish in social situations, and they frequently look for adventure and enjoyment.

4. Agreeableness: Empathic, cooperative, and sympathetic people are agreeable. They emphasize social care and friendliness, show altruistic impulses, and appreciate peace in relationships.

5. Emotional Stability or Neuroticism: Neuroticism is a reflection of emotional stability or lack of it. People with high neuroticism are more sensitive to emotions, anxious, and prone to mood swings; people with low neuroticism are typically more stable and steadfast.

Comprehending these characteristics can offer an all-encompassing perspective on an individual's personality, illuminating their incentives, manner of communication, and social interactions.

Different Personality Types According to the Myers-Briggs Type Indicator (MBTI)

Numerous personality typing systems provide extra viewpoints for comprehending human behavior in addition to the Big Five. The Myers-Briggs Type Indicator (MBTI) is one such tool that divides people into 16 different personality types using four partitions:

1. Intuition (N) versus Sensing (S)

2. Introversion (I) versus Extraversion (E)

3. Judging (J) versus Perceiving (P)

4. Thinking (T) versus Feeling (F)

An INFJ (Introverted, Intuitive, Feeling, Judging) person, for instance, is typically inventive, introspective, empathic, and well-organized. By identifying and valuing each person's distinctive qualities, interests, and communication styles, a genuine relationship can be fostered through the appreciation of these personality types.

Recognizing Four Typical Temperamental Features

The term "temperament" describes innate, physiologically derived behavioral and emotional patterns. Temperament is intimately linked to personality, but it focuses more on intrinsic inclinations that develop early in life and affect how people respond to different circumstances. Four typical characteristics of temperament include:

1. Activity Level: This characteristic relates to an individual's innate energy level and propensity for both mental and physical endeavors. While some people are very busy and thrive in fast-paced surroundings, others are more content to sit quietly and think things out.

2. Sociability: Sociability is a measure of how comfortable and happy a person is in social situations. While some people are naturally friendly and very social, others enjoy privacy or small groups of people.

3. Emotional Reactivity: The frequency and depth of an emotional response to a stimulus are referred to as emotional reactivity. While some people are very

reactive and feel intense emotions rapidly, others are more emotionally stable and remain so even under difficult situations.

4. Adaptability: This refers to the ease with which an individual adjusts to novel circumstances, changes in surroundings, and unforeseen events. While some people are adaptable and resilient and see change as a chance for personal development, others may find change difficult and would much rather remain in the same place.

We can appreciate other people's points of view, adjust our associations accordingly, and create lasting relationships that are based on respect and understanding when we are aware of temperamental variations.

Understanding personality types and temperaments is essential to developing genuine relationships. We can establish environments that respect each person's distinct character and foster meaningful interactions based on understanding, empathy, and friendship by accepting diversity and valuing the richness of human differences.

CHAPTER FOUR

The Necessity of Gaining Mastery of Emotional Intelligence

Emotional intelligence is among the most important abilities we need to cultivate if we want to get to know someone completely and have a meaningful relationship with them. This chapter explores the complex web of emotions, how they affect relationships, and the basic ways we might develop emotional awareness to strengthen our bonds with one another.

Four Essential Guidelines for Comprehending Emotions

Our experiences and relationships are shaped by the vibrant strands of emotions that permeate our lives. They are the murmurs of our inner selves, voicing our most secret hopes, anxieties, pleasures, and grief. Comprehending emotions is akin to interpreting an intricate vernacular that reveals a great deal about our identities and worldviews. Here are four essential guidelines for comprehending emotions:

1. The Emotional Spectrum: Each emotion has its own distinct energy and message and ranges widely from joy and happiness to rage and grief. Acknowledging and classifying these feelings improves our self-awareness and increases our capacity for empathy with the feelings of others.

2. The Power of Empathy: The foundation of emotional intelligence is empathy. It is the capacity to put oneself in another person's position, experience their emotions, and react to them with empathy. By validating the feelings of others, we build trust and strengthen our bonds with them.

3. Emotions in Interaction: Emotions are important in interaction because they affect how we express ourselves and understand what other people are saying. Effective communication can be encouraged and misunderstandings can be avoided by being conscious of our emotional drives and engaging in active listening.

4. Emotional Regulation: Those who are emotionally intelligent are adept at controlling their emotions and expressing themselves in constructive ways. This entails being aware of when feelings are getting out of control, exercising self-control, and looking for healthy ways to express yourself.

Four Essential Elements for Growing in Emotional Awareness

The cornerstone of emotional intelligence is emotional awareness. It entails becoming aware of our emotions, comprehending where they come from, and utilizing this knowledge to handle relationships in a genuine manner. These four elements are essential for cultivating emotional awareness:

1. Self-Reflection: By regularly reflecting on ourselves, we can examine our emotional conditions, spot reoccurring patterns, and obtain an understanding of our central ideas and values. This introspective process can be aided by mindfulness exercises, and keeping a journal.

2. Empathy Training: Mastering nonverbal clue reading, listening without passing judgment, and validating the experiences of others are all part of developing empathy. Empathy training, role-playing practices, and thought-provoking dialogues all help to build this crucial ability.

3. Emotional Literacy: Increasing our understanding of emotions improves our ability to express complex emotions and interact with others. Our emotional

literacy is enhanced by reading books, going to emotional intelligence seminars, and having candid conversations relating to the subject of emotions.

4. Resolving Conflict: Resilience and emotional awareness are necessary when viewing conflict as a chance for personal development. Relationships are strengthened and constructive communication is encouraged when disagreements are approached with empathy, active listening, and a desire to appreciate different points of view.

We go on a life-changing path of self-discovery and genuine relationships with others when we become competent in emotional intelligence and cultivate emotional awareness. We build deeper, more meaningful connections based on empathy and originality as we learn more about the complexities of emotions and their effects.

CHAPTER FIVE

The Relevance of Beliefs, Values, and Worldviews

Among the most significant aspects we come across in our quest to get to know someone well is their worldview, values, and beliefs. These factors influence a person's identity, choices, and relationships with others and the outside environment. Not only can mastering them improve our relationships, but it also promotes respect, empathy, and sincere relationships.

The Cornerstone of Identity

Values and beliefs serve as the cornerstone of a person's identity. They are the firmly held beliefs and ideals that direct one's actions, ideas, and feelings. Beliefs can range from views about social justice to confidence in a higher force. They might be intellectual, religious, or private. Contrarily, values are the principles and standards that one uses to determine what matters and has significance in life, like success, kindness, or honesty.

Being sensitive and receptive is necessary when examining someone's beliefs and values. Listening, inquiring, and attempting to comprehend the rationale behind their convictions are more important than passing judgment or forcing our own opinions on others. Beliefs and values are frequently shaped by an individual's life history, childhood, culture, and introspection. Through exploring these facets, we acquire a deep understanding of what is important to people.

Discovering Core Beliefs

Finding out someone's underlying beliefs — the guiding ideas that influence their behavior and worldview — is essential to getting to know them well. Fundamental beliefs serve as people's lenses through which they view the world, other people, and themselves. They have an impact on mindset, understanding, and reactions to opportunities and problems in life.

Core beliefs can be restrictive or uplifting. People who have strong core beliefs are more resilient, self-assured, and driven. Restricting core beliefs, however, can lead to fear, self-doubt, and obstacles to personal development. A very good example of uplifting and restrictive core beliefs are "I am qualified and worthy of success" and "I am undesirable and undeserving" respectively.

We can thoughtfully probe people's core beliefs during significant conversations by posing probing queries like these:

Which values are most important to you? Can I know how your beliefs affect the way you make decisions? Could you describe a memorable event that changed the way you saw the world?

We establish an atmosphere of originality and openness by paying close attention to what they have to say and appreciating the importance of their convictions. This deepens our bond with them.

Accepting Various Worldviews

Broader viewpoints on existence, truth, and the universe are included in worldviews. Ideological, philosophical, theological, and cultural influences all have an impact on them. Building appropriate, peaceful relationships requires an understanding of other people's worldviews, particularly in today's global and collaborative world.

Managing disparate worldviews calls for humility, curiosity, and an openness to new ideas. We can welcome differences as chances for mutual understanding and development rather than seeing them as barriers. We can broaden our own perspective and improve our relationships with others by investigating and appreciating many points of view.

There are four essential methods for negotiating different worldviews:

1. Fostering Empathy: Consider other people from their point of view in order to comprehend their worldview.

2. Active Listening: Pay close attention, free from bias, and make an effort to understand the fundamental values and convictions.

3. Locating Points of Agreement: To overcome ideological or cultural disparity, concentrate on common values and objectives.

4. Study Constantly: To increase your comprehension of many worldviews, pursue lifelong study.

Culturally, religiously, and philosophically, we open the door to genuine relationships by valuing diversity and the complexity of human life.

In summary, learning about someone's beliefs, values, and worldviews is like learning about the layers of a gorgeous tapestry as regards the art of truly connecting with others; each thread is distinct yet adds to the magnificence of the overall picture. By exploring these many facets of identity, we broaden our perspectives, develop empathy, and foster real relationships.

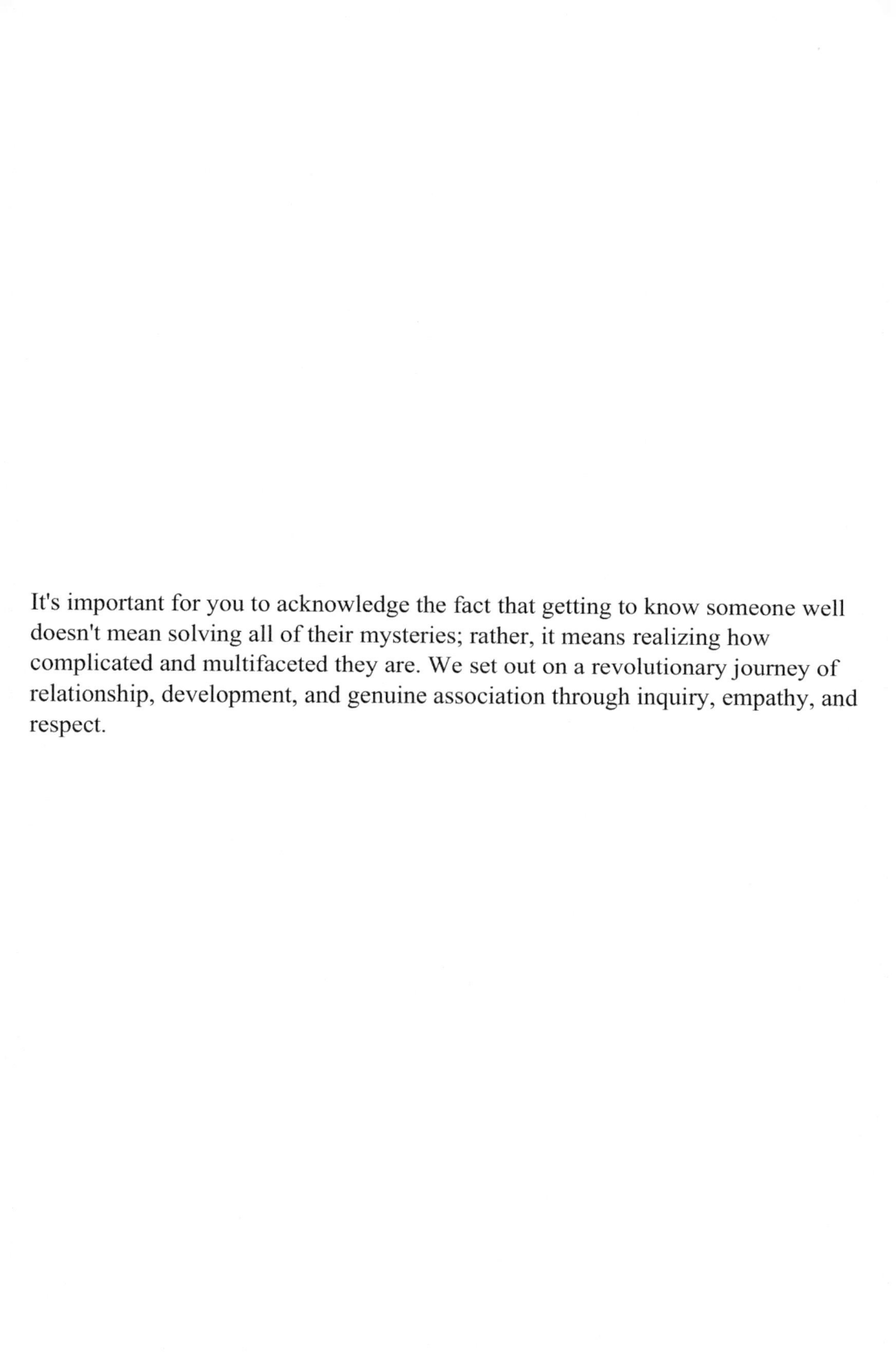

It's important for you to acknowledge the fact that getting to know someone well doesn't mean solving all of their mysteries; rather, it means realizing how complicated and multifaceted they are. We set out on a revolutionary journey of relationship, development, and genuine association through inquiry, empathy, and respect.

CHAPTER SIX

The Fundamental Knowledge of Communication Styles

The foundation of every relationship is communication. It involves more than just words, rather the way in which those words are spoken, heard, and perceived. This chapter will examine the many communication styles that individuals display and how comprehending them can improve relationships.

The Four Fundamental Communication Principles

Let's establish four fundamental communication principles before delving into the specifics of various communication styles:

1. Active Listening: The foundation of successful communication is active listening. It entails not just listening to what someone has to say but also comprehending their viewpoint, emotions, and goals.

2. Empathy: Profound communication requires the ability to put oneself in the other person's shoes. Greater intimacy and understanding are fostered by empathy.

3. Nonverbal Communication: In the field of communication, you should be aware that language is only one component of the picture. Communication also includes gesticulations, intonation, body posture, and facial expressions.

4. Cultural Sensitivity: Individuals from various origins may have unique communication styles that are shaped by their experiences, childhood, and traditions. Effective communication requires sensitivity to these distinctions.

Four Fundamental Styles of Communication

1. Assertive Communication: In this form of communication, ideas, emotions, and opinions are expressed politely and clearly. Assertive communicators lack aggression and are straightforward, honest, and self-assured. They respect other individual's rights and cherish their own rights as well.

2. Passive Communication: People who practice passive communication shy away from confrontation and put peace before their own demands. They could find it difficult to stand up for themselves or say no, which frequently results in emotions of bitterness or being a pushover.

3. Aggressive Communication: People who communicate aggressively are frequently harsh, demanding, and rude. They may employ coercion or intimidation techniques, put their own wants ahead of those of others, and amplify disagreements rather than find a solution.

4. Passive-Aggressive Communication: In this form of communication, aspects of the passive and aggressive modes of communication are blended to create a different style. Although they may come off as cooperative on the outside, those who are passive-aggressive may be subtly or indirectly expressing their hatred, sarcasm, or anger.

Four Basic Ways of Discovering Typical Styles of Communication

Gaining an understanding of these styles can enable you to conduct discussions more skillfully:

a. Assertive: Seek straightforward communication, adherence to comfort zone, and an emphasis on finding solutions rather than criticism.

b. Passive: Keep an eye out for hesitation to voice thoughts, a hard time saying no, and a predisposition to steer clear of conflict by any means.

c. Aggressive: Take note of harsh language, failure to empathize with others, command over discussions, and an emphasis on being victorious or correct.

d. Passive-Aggressive: Watch out for behaviors that conceal genuine emotions, sarcasm, insincere compliments, and veiled insults.

Three Strategies to Modify Your Style of Communication

Changing the way you communicate can improve how you engage with other people:

a. Flexibility: Be prepared to modify your communication style according to the circumstance and the other person. In the workplace, for instance, you should be more assertive, but while helping a buddy in need, you should be more understanding and patient.

b. Active Listening: Before answering someone, engage in active listening to fully comprehend the viewpoint of the individual. This promotes civil discourse and demonstrates regard.

c. Empathy: Develop empathy by taking into account the thoughts, emotions, and goals of the other person. This helps to establish a true association that is rooted in trust.

Beating Four Typical Communication Obstacles

Although it's not always easy, effective communication is worthwhile. Here are four typical obstacles along with solutions:

1. Misunderstandings: Make your message clear, seek clarification by asking questions, and refrain from assuming anything.

2. Emotional Barriers: To stop arguments from getting worse, control your emotions, maintain composure, and get some rest when necessary.

3. Cultural Differences: Endeavor to be inquisitive and courteous in regard to cultural differences, and pursue understanding by posing questions instead of passing judgment.

4. Lack of Trust: Establish trust in the course of time by being dependable, communicating in an honest and reliable manner, and honoring your word.

In summary, communication methods are as varied as the people who employ them. You can build stronger, more cogent relationships by identifying, comprehending, and adjusting your own style besides being aware of others' types. Relaying information is only one aspect of effective communication; another is fostering relationships based on empathy, respect, and sincere comprehension.

CHAPTER SEVEN

Developing Trust and Vulnerability

Two of the most important characteristics in the pursuit of getting to know someone deeply are trust and vulnerability. They are the strands that bind deep connections together and promote intimacy, understanding, and bonding. This chapter delves into the complexities of developing trust and accepting vulnerability, examining their significance in the skill of authentic human relations.

The Four Bases of Trust

The foundation of any worthwhile relationship is trust. It is the conviction that someone is trustworthy, moral, and sincere. Building trust requires consistent behavior, honest communication, and shared experiences — all of which take time to develop. The four bases of trust are as follows:

1. Genuineness: Establishing trust requires being genuine. We encourage others to reciprocate when we present as our genuine selves, without any form of pretense. Since genuineness denotes sincerity and openness, trust is fostered by it.

2. Reliability: Eventually, trust is cultivated through verbal and behavioral consistency. People realize they can rely on us when we fulfill our word, maintain our half of the bargain, and exhibit dependability. This creates a more solid relationship that is anchored on trust.

3. Open conversation: By establishing a secure environment for expression, candid and open conversation promotes trust. Trust grows when we communicate honestly, listen intently, and resolve problems in a positive way.

4. Respect and Comfort Zone: Trust cannot exist without honoring the privacy and comfort zone of others. We show respect for others when we respect their choices, feelings, and privacy. This creates an environment where trust can grow.

The Four Main Purposes of Vulnerability

Although the vulnerability is sometimes misinterpreted as a weakness, it is actually a powerful quality that strengthens bonds and encourages empathy. Adopting vulnerability is letting ourselves be visualized and perceived in a genuine way by being honest and open about our ideas, feelings, worries, and goals. The following are the four main purposes of vulnerability in a deep relationship:

1. Authentic Sharing: When we confide in reliable people, a bridge to empathy and understanding is built. It makes it possible for people to see past our outward appearance and promotes deeper relationships built on sincere acceptance.

2. Empathy and Connectivity: When we accept our own vulnerability, we open the door for others to follow suit. This shared vulnerability strengthens the link between people by fostering empathy, understanding, and a feeling of our common humanity.

3. Fearless Dialogs: Being vulnerable entails fearlessly participating in challenging dialogues. We make room for genuine communication and mutual development when we are open and honest in expressing our wants, interests, and feelings.

4. Developing Emotional Closeness: Being vulnerable is the first step toward emotional closeness. In relationships, we foster a deep sense of connection and compassion when we openly and honestly express our deepest thoughts and emotions.

Six Essential Steps to Foster Trust and Vulnerability

Intention, perseverance, and action are necessary for the continuous processes of fostering trust and accepting vulnerability. The following six actions will help you foster these vital components in your relationships:

1. Engage in Active Listening: Pay close attention to the experiences, emotions, and viewpoints of people without passing judgment or interjecting. Acknowledge and express empathy for their feelings.

2. Be Truthful and Open: Express your ideas, emotions, and goals in a genuine and truthful manner. Don't conceal or withhold information that might undermine confidence.

3. Respect Boundaries: Clearly express your personal boundaries while also honoring those of others. Understand that establishing trust and preserving healthy relationships depends on acknowledging boundaries.

4. Exhibit Consistency: Act and speak in a consistent manner. To gain and sustain trust, fulfill obligations, honor pledges, and exhibit dependability.

5. Develop Self-Awareness: Consider your own weaknesses, phobias, and stressors. Gain self-awareness to see in what way your words and deeds affect the vulnerability and trust of other people.

6. Accept Imperfection: Admit that no one is flawless and that flaws are a necessary component of being human. Accept the opportunities for personal development and connection that come with having flaws and vulnerabilities.

You make room for more relevant relationships, sincere understanding, and stronger connections by valuing vulnerability and building trust. It's important for you to acknowledge the fact that genuine intimacy arises from the bravery to exhibit vulnerability and authenticity, establishing areas where emotions collide and spirits reunite.

CHAPTER EIGHT

Developing Empathy and Compassion

Empathy and compassion constitute the crucial aspects of deep understanding and bonding in the elaborate subject of human relations. They are the links that connect our hearts, enabling us to truly relate and get to know people on a deep level. This chapter will examine the practice of developing empathy and compassion, focusing on the fundamentals of empathetic listening, as well as, the relationship-changing potential of compassion.

The capacity to comprehend and experience another person's emotions is known as empathy. It is an astounding realization of the human nature we all share, rising above simple sympathy or pity. We must first allow ourselves to be genuinely receptive to others in order to develop empathy.

Five Essential Guidelines for Empathetic Listening

Deep relationships are built on the foundation of empathic listening. It entails hearing what someone says, as well as, comprehending the motivations, feelings, and viewpoints that lie behind those words. The following are five fundamentals of empathetic listening:

1. Presence: Anytime someone is talking to you, give them your whole attention. Set away any outside distractions and focus entirely.

2. Openness: Enter into discussions without any preconceived notions. Be prepared to let go of your biases and preconceptions.

3. Non-Judgment: Listen to reason and refrain from drawing hasty judgments. Give the other individual the freedom to air their views without worrying about backlash.

4. Validation: Even when you dispute with someone, respect their experiences and feelings. Acknowledge the importance and validity of their feelings.

5. Reflective Listening: To make sure you grasp what you've heard, reflect it back. Use phrases to express back the thing you've understood from your counterpart, so he can validate your perception or provide a clearer explanation.

Empathetic listening fosters a safe environment in which people feel comfortable sharing their deepest feelings. This increases our comprehension of them as individuals and builds trust.

Five Techniques for Developing Compassion

Empathy in operation is compassion. It is the sincere desire to lessen pain and advance other people's comfort. Our relationships become loving, supportive bonds when we practice compassion in them. Here are five strategies for developing compassion:

1. Practice Empathy: Take part in activities that help you become more empathic like putting yourself in another person's shoes or thinking back on typical human situations.

2. Self-Compassion: Learn to have empathy for yourself and acknowledge that you are also worthy of compassion and understanding.

3. Acts of Kindness: Be kind and giving to others, whether it be by tiny tokens or significant deeds.

4. Forgiveness: Work on forgiving yourself as well as other people. Compassion can grow when old grudges and resentments are released.

5. Mindful Awareness: Develop a consciousness of your feelings, ideas, and responses. You can respond to others less reactively and more compassionately when you are conscious of your feelings, ideas, and responses.

Five Strategies for Including Compassion and Empathy in Your Relationships:

Compassion and empathy complement in strengthening our bonds with one another. Empathic listening allows us to comprehend the feelings that are conveyed through words. Furthermore, when we react compassionately, we significantly provide care and assistance. Here are five strategies for incorporating compassion and empathy into your relationships:

1. Listen from the Heart: Try to listen with empathy in every interaction, making an effort to comprehend everything that is said and how it is felt.

2. React Kindly: Show sympathy and kindness in response to someone who shares their pleasures or hardships. Provide words of support or useful assistance.

3. Show Vulnerability: Genuinely communicate your personal feelings and experiences. Being vulnerable encourages empathy and draws people's compassion.

4. Practice Forgiveness: Choose to forgive and forge ahead with compassion rather than holding grudges and passing judgment.

5. Develop Empathy Every Day: Exercise empathy and compassion every day in your relationships with people and with yourself.

Empathy and compassion are the keys that open doors to genuine, long-lasting relationships. We are able to see outward manifestations and establish a connection with the core of people. By doing this, we improve not just our own lives but also the lives of others around us, establishing a society based on compassion, empathy, and sincere human relations.

CHAPTER NINE

The Necessity of Settling Conflict Effectively

Every significant relationship will inevitably involve conflict. Disagreements and differences of opinion are inevitable while dealing with romantic partners, friends, family, or coworkers. The way we manage and settle these disputes says a lot about the degree and development of our bonds. We'll explore the skill of effective conflict resolution in this chapter, transforming uneasy situations into chances for development and greater appreciation.

Mastering the Basic Idea of Conflict

Understanding the nature of conflicts is a necessary first step towards finding an effective solution. Dissimilarities in viewpoints, values, interests, or desires frequently lead to conflict. These distinctions are the things that make people distinctive; they are not intrinsically bad. Conflicts can worsen when these disparities collide, though, if they are not handled correctly.

It's important to keep in mind that conflict does not equate to animosity. Conflicts can be handled with empathy, respect, and a sincere effort to comprehend one another's perspectives. Instead of attempting to subjugate or control the other side, settlement of conflict is about identifying common ground and coming up with mutual agreement.

Seven Techniques for Settling Conflicts

1. Active Listening: Active listening is the cornerstone of conflict settlement. This entails focusing entirely on the other person and not thinking about your answer or interjecting while they are speaking. Whether you disagree with them, acknowledge their thoughts and feelings to demonstrate empathy.

2. Expressing Your Emotions: Use "I" statements rather than accusing language to boldly and plainly communicate your own desires and emotions. For instance, you may say, "I feel ignored anytime my opinions are rejected," as opposed to, "You constantly neglect my opinions."

3. Pursuing Understanding: Give careful thought to the fundamental causes of the disagreement. Which fundamental values or desires are experiencing a conflict? Conflicts can occasionally be the outward sign of more serious problems that require attention.

4. Discovering Common Ground: Search for points of concession or agreement. Concentrate on common objectives or principles that can act as a basis for settling the dispute. Collaborating to generate ideas can be a very powerful tool for generating aesthetic results.

5. Controlling Emotions: Although emotions can intensify at the time of disagreements, it's important to maintain composure. Before carrying on with the conversation, engage in emotional control practices like deep breathing, meditation, or utilizing a temporary pause to calm up.

6. Collaborative Problem-Solving: See conflict not as a rivalry but as a cooperative process for solving problems. Collaborate to generate ideas for solutions that take into account the desires and worries of both sides. Be eager to make changes and receptive to criticism.

7. Seeking Third-Party Mediation if Needed: If communication has been shattered or emotions are too strong, there are situations when third-party mediation may be necessary. A third-party mediator can assist in encouraging fruitful communication and assisting the parties in reaching a settlement.

Five Ways of Turning Conflict into Chances for Relationship and Personal Development

Although disputes can be difficult, they also offer priceless chances for relationship and personal development. Here are five strategies for using disagreements as drivers for improvement:

1. Deeper Understanding: Resolving disagreements helps you understand both the other person and yourself better. You develop deeper empathy and a stronger sense of connection as you get to know one another's triggers, manner of communication, and sensitive regions.

2. Better Communication Skills: Engaging in conflict settlement exercises your ability to speak clearly, listen intently, and handle uncomfortable situations with tact and grace.

3. Establishing Trust: Settling disagreements amicably fosters resilience and trust in interpersonal relationships. Common respect and trust are strengthened when both sides recognize that disagreements can be resolved amicably and maturely.

4. Cognitive Proficiency: Settling conflicts promotes original thought and cognitive proficiency. It pushes you to think outside the box and come up with ideas that work for everyone.

5. Personal Development: Ultimately, handling conflict calls for emotional intelligence, self-awareness, and a readiness to change and advance. It's a chance for self-improvement and personal progress as you consider your own responses and actions.

In summary, developing authentic relationships and getting to know someone well requires the ability to settle conflict. You may turn troubled moments into opportunities for greater understanding, personal development, and deeper bonds by addressing disagreements with empathy, effective listening, and a team-oriented perspective.

CHAPTER TEN

The Value of Forgiveness and Restoration in Relationships

Forgiveness and restoration are strands that deeply link us together in the complex web of human interactions. They serve as the links that help us get beyond hurt, betrayal, and misunderstandings and move toward more meaningful relationships and comprehension. We will examine the transformational value of forgiveness and healing in this chapter, as well as how these concepts are essential to getting to know someone well and developing a true relationship with them.

Basic Knowledge of Forgiveness

Being able to forgive is a great act of bravery and compassion, not just a way to let go of the past or forget wrongs. By letting go of our grudges and anger, forgiveness allows us to move on to restoration and harmony. But forgiving does not imply supporting bad behavior or absolving wrongdoing. It's about admitting the hurt, realizing the consequences, and making the decision to release the emotional weight that binds us to bygone days.

Forgiveness is not merely a gift we render to other people, but a gift we render to ourselves as well. It frees us from the vicious cycle of resentment and gives us the opportunity to regain our emotional stability and inner serenity. Forgiveness is a crucial component in relationships because it makes it possible for bonds to grow and trust to be restored. Empathy, openness, and a readiness to adopt vulnerability are necessary to establish forgiveness. We must also be willing to acknowledge our own frailty and provide compassion to people who have wronged us.

The Road to Restoration

The process of restoration is complex and involves spiritual, psychological, and emotional aspects. It is a rejuvenation and repair process that leads us to unity and stability. When we face our emotional hurt with tenderness and truthfulness, self-awareness, and self-compassion are the first steps toward restoration. It entails confronting the suffering directly, admitting how it affects our lives, and asking for help and direction when we need it.

Restoration in relationships is a team effort that calls for tolerance, sensitivity, and understanding on both sides. It entails establishing secure environments for open dialogue, allowing people to express their feelings honestly, and paying attention to one another's viewpoints. Restoration is a nonlinear process that is filled with obstacles and disappointments as well as moments of progress and development.

Reestablishing Trust

Genuine relationships are based on a foundation of trust. It is the conviction that someone else is trustworthy, moral, and kind. Reestablishing trust after it has been damaged by treachery, deceit, or disagreement takes time, work, and sincere repentance. Although it is difficult to reclaim, trust can be earned again.

Frankness and responsibility are the first steps in restoring trust. It entails owning up to our mistakes, admitting the suffering we have initiated, and, if at all feasible, making apologies. Honesty, persistence, and a dedication to open communication are further requirements for trust. It is developed by tiny deeds of compassion, empathy, and kindness that show a real desire to mend and build the connection.

The Importance of Forgiveness and Restoration in Getting to Know Someone Deeply

To truly know someone is to accept their human nature, complexity, and frailties. It is to discern beyond names and passing appearances to the depth of their experiences, feelings, and beliefs. A crucial part of this process is forgiveness and restoration, which enable us to get past the layers of hurt, miscommunication, and strife that frequently hide our genuine relationships.

By forgiving others, we make room for compassion and empathy to grow. We welcome a deeper comprehension of one another's viewpoints and experiences by relinquishing judgments and assumptions. Conversely, restoration encourages development and resilience, giving us the ability to overcome past traumas and create deeper, more genuine associations.

Forgiveness and restoration are guiding concepts in the art of genuine human relations; they show us the way toward intimacy and association. They serve as a reminder of our common humanity, our empathetic nature, and our intrinsic capacity for transformation and restoration. We can create atmospheres of trust, tolerance, and love in our relationships by adopting forgiveness and restoration, which allows for the growth of genuine understanding and deep relationships.

CHAPTER ELEVEN

Mutual Development in a Relationship

The mutual development that happens over time is possibly the most satisfying part of getting to know someone deeply. Relationships have the special ability to mold, stretch, and develop us into superior models of ourselves. We'll explore the skill of developing enduring relationships, encouraging one another's personal development, and supporting one another's progress in this chapter.

Three Crucial Elements for Promoting Mutual Development in Relationships

Sincere relationships are based on mutual development. A progressive and complementing relationship arises when two people join together with the intention of learning from one another, sharing experiences, and developing together. These three factors are essential for promoting reciprocal development in relationships:

1. Openness or Vulnerability: Nurturing mutual development in a relationship requires openness. It all comes down to having the courage to open up to the other person about your emotions, ideas, and experiences. This openness makes room for profound comprehension and empathy to grow. Openness or vulnerability allows people to explore fresh viewpoints and concepts, which promotes individual and group development.

2. Accepting Differences in Human Characters: Relationships benefit from diversity. Every individual contributes their distinct upbringing, convictions, and

life experiences. Accepting these distinctions promotes a respectful and educational environment as well as a rich interchange of views. Consider differences as chances for understanding and progress rather than as obstacles.

3. Common Objectives and Visions: It's critical to agree on common objectives and visions as a relationship develops. This could involve goals for one's own private life or profession, as well as common interests like travel or artistic endeavors. When both parties are pursuing common objectives, they encourage and assist one another, advancing their own development.

Three Methods for Developing Prolonged Relationships

Maintenance and awareness are necessary for long-term relationships. They require attention, endurance, and work to flourish, much like gardens. The following three tactics can help you develop meaningful and enduring relationships:

1. Maintaining Consistent Communication: In any relationship, communication is essential. It's important to set aside time for in-depth discussions in which you actively listen to the other person, share your opinions honestly, and seem really interested in their life. Maintaining a profound relationship requires regular check-ins, whether by phone conversations, messages, or in-person convenes.

2. Great Time Together: Spending quality time together promotes the creation of enduring memories, fostering stronger relationships. Whether it's taking up new hobbies, experiencing the outdoors, or just spending time together relaxing, plan things that you both like. These mutual experiences strengthen your bond and foster intimacy.

3. Empathy and Tolerance: The foundation of meaningful relationships is empathy. Consider the other person's point of view, make an effort to comprehend it, and provide them emotional support. Offer empathy and assistance at trying times, and fervently acknowledge and applaud their accomplishments.

Three Strategies to Encourage Relationship Development and Progress

A basic component of getting to know someone well is encouraging their personal development. The following three strategies can help you spur each other's development on the private and business fronts:

1. Encouragement or Motivation: Give them words of support and inspiration as they work toward their objectives. Be their supporter by recognizing their accomplishments and encouraging them when they face obstacles. Your faith in their potential might bolster their self-assurance and tenacity.

2. Give Constructive Feedback: Progress requires constructive criticism. Provide constructive criticism in an encouraging and non-judgmental way, emphasizing areas that need work and making recommendations for advancement. Be open to feedback as well so you can encourage a culture of ongoing learning and development.

3. Establish a Learning Environment: Encourage a growth mentality in the association. Exchange information, materials, and experiences that advance one another's education. Take part in thought-provoking conversations, confront one another's viewpoints, and jointly investigate novel concepts.

In summary, developing a relationship with another person is a wonderful and life-changing event. It's about valuing openness, cultivating relationships, and encouraging one another's personal development. A profoundly meaningful and rewarding relationship path can be paved with mutual understanding, acknowledging diversity, and encouraging a culture of gaining wisdom.

CONCLUSION

This book provides a helpful guide through the complex world of interpersonal relationships. We have looked at the significance of supporting genuine relationships and investigating the essence of what makes each person special during the course of this book.

Real relationships are built on the fundamental ideas covered in this short guide, which range from openness and tolerance to active listening and empathy. In addition to improving our own lives, we also forge enduring relationships with people by acknowledging and appreciating individuals for what they are and not what we wish them to be.

As we end this chapter, let's continue our dedication to developing real relationships that are based on common recognition, trust, and a profound understanding of one another's real natures. We discover genuine satisfaction and the hidden wealth of knowledge in our individual experiences through genuine relationships, so may we never give up on the pursuit of building genuine relationships by knowing people deeply and allowing them to know us as well.

ABOUT THE AUTHOR

James Edwards was born on May 16th, 1974. He suffered from schizophrenia in the year 1998, which threatened to ruin his mental health. It happened that when James Edwards was miraculously healed of his mental sickness in the year 2012, he decided to serve mankind with his mental prowess. He does rigorous research on relevant subject matters and documents his discoveries in the form of concise and clear short nonfiction books.

"FINANCIAL LITERACY FOR TEENS AND YOUNG ADULTS" is one of his popular books. Other books include "UNDERSTANDING MEDICAL TERMINOLOGY BY MASTERING PREFIX AND SUFFIX," "LOWER CHOLESTEROL NATURALLY," and "A SHORT DESCRIPTION OF THE SECRET OF RELIEVING PAIN BY TRAINING YOUR NERVOUS SYSTEM DIFFERENTLY." He is a prolific author of plenty of short nonfiction books. Every word James writes is infused with his genuine desire to positively impact every reader's life and his passion for personal progress.

Start reading James Edwards's books now to begin your road toward a more purposeful and happy existence.

You can discover his other useful and highly interesting short books by visiting his author central page here: https://www.amazon.com/author/jamesedwards1974

Printed in Great Britain
by Amazon